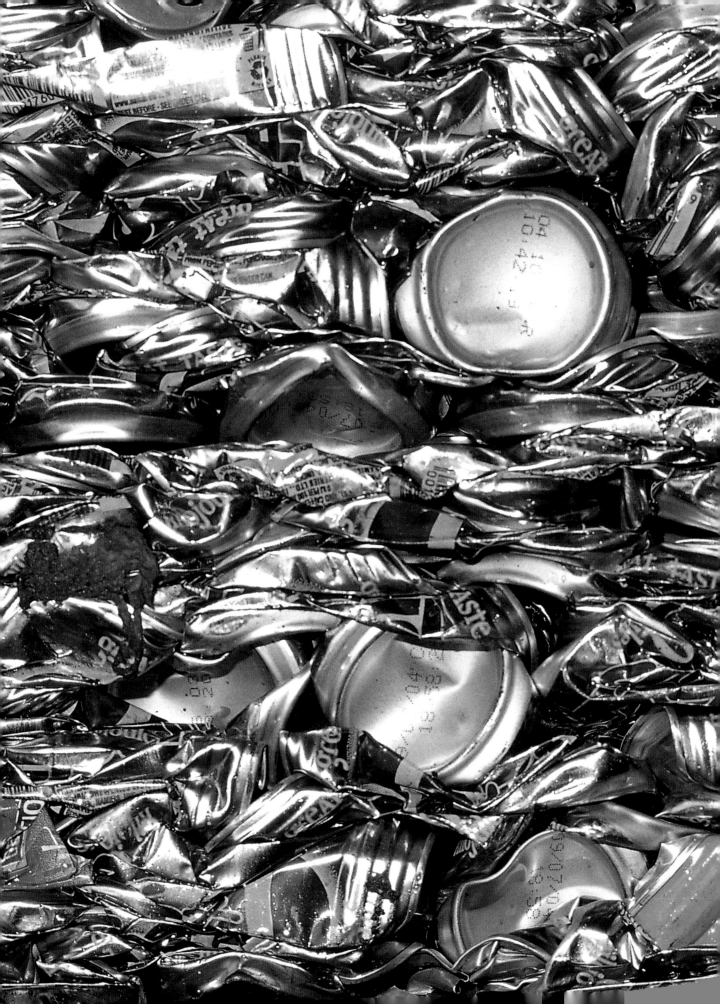

recycling & reusing

Metal

Ruth Thomson

Photography by Neil Thomson

A+
Smart Apple Media

First published in 2006 by Franklin Watts
338 Euston Road, London NW1 3BH

Franklin Watts Australia, Hachette Children's Books
Level 17/207 Kent Street, Sydney NSW 2000

Editor: Rachel Cooke, Design: Holly Mann, Art Director: Rachel Hamdi,
Consultant: Diana Caldwell, Novelis

Additional photography
Franklin Watts 6bl, 6c, 6br, 7, 9r; Atlas Copco 8br; B.H.P. Billiton 8tr, 8bl; Recycle now 14tl, 26br,
27bl; Novelis 15bl, 15tr, 15cr, 15br; Ecoscene/Richard Glover 9l, Ecoscene/Miroslav Imbrisevic 26t.

Published in the United States by Smart Apple Media
2140 Howard Drive West, North Mankato, Minnesota 56003

Library of Congress Cataloging-in-Publication Data

Thomson, Ruth, 1949-
Metal / by Ruth Thomson.
p. cm. — (Recycling and reusing)
Includes index.
ISBN-13: 978-1-58340-937-4
1. Metals—Juvenile literature. I. Title.

TA459.T49 2006
669'.042—dc22   2006000019

9 8 7 6 5 4 3 2 1

Contents

What is metal like?

Think how useful metal is. We travel in cars, trains, and airplanes made of metal. Industries, hospitals, and building sites use metal machines. Our homes are filled with metal sinks, ovens, and radiators. There are more than 70 types of metal.

Steel is hard and very strong. It is used for bridges, machines, and beams for buildings.

Steel can be sharpened to make tools.

A steel knife has a sharp blade for cutting.

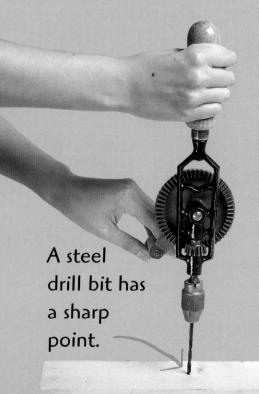

A steel drill bit has a sharp point.

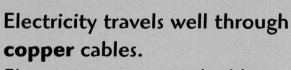

Electricity travels well through **copper** cables. Electricity comes into buildings along copper cables. Plastic, which does not **conduct** electricity, covers the wires.

Aluminum and steel can be rolled into thin, light sheets. The sheets are made into strong food and drink cans.

Heat travels very quickly through metals.
Metal pots and pans heat up over a flame. They are useful for cooking food.

Gold, silver, and **platinum** are rare precious metals. Jewelers use precious metals to make rings, necklaces, bracelets, earrings, and brooches.

Turned to rust

Most **iron** and steel things rust if they are left out in the rain. They turn brown and flaky and begin to crumble into pieces.

Mining for metals

Most metals are found inside rocks. **Geologists** search for areas where rocks contain a lot of metal. These rocks are known as **ores**.

Metal-bearing rock

Open pit mining

If the ore is near the surface, huge **excavators** remove the top layers of soil and rock and then scoop up the ore. Sometimes explosives blast hard ore into pieces.

Underground mining

Some ores lie deep underground. Miners dig a deep shaft with tunnels leading from it. They drill or blast the rocks to mine the ore.

As the wheel of the excavator turns, the scoops pick up ore.

Making iron

Iron is the most plentiful metal produced. Iron ore is crushed and heated with **coke** and **limestone** in a **blast furnace** to separate the metal. Iron cracks easily, so it is used to make steel, which is much stronger.

Making steel

Molten iron is poured over scrap steel in a huge, tilting container. A jet of pure oxygen blasts onto the liquid metal. This burns away most of the impurities to make steel.

9

Saving metal

Most metal objects are durable and long-lasting. Things that one person no longer wants are usually in good enough condition for someone else to reuse.

For sale

All of these secondhand metal items were on sale in a market. Can you recognize them all?

Old oil drums

People find all sorts of uses for empty oil drums.

Animal feed trough

Road Closed
No access to NY3.
Use NY50.

Temporary road sign

USE ME

Litter bin

Any old iron?

In many parts of the world, collectors wander city streets, buying any bits of old metal they find. They take the metal to a scrapyard.

A metal scrapyard

Scrap metal merchants sort the metal before they resell it. Builders buy pipes, rods, girders, and gates. Craftworkers buy pieces of scrap metal to **melt** and shape into furniture, mirror frames, and other objects.

Remade metal

In many countries, small metal workshops turn old **factory**-made objects into new, cheap household equipment.

Pots, pans, and stoves

In Morocco, metalworkers cut old steel water heaters and oil drums in half.

They attach legs to make charcoal stoves.

They cut and shape pieces to make buckets.

They add handles to turn them into huge cooking pots.

An original oven

A washing machine drum has been turned into this portable oven. The food vendor bakes sweet potatoes in it.

A glass holder

Factories often bind **bales** of goods with long metal strips. Once the bales are opened, the strips are thrown away. In Egypt, craftspeople reuse them to make holders for carrying glasses of hot tea.

Bicycle chain bits

Factories press bicycle chains out of metal sheets. The leftover sheets are full of holes. These are of no use to the factories, but metal craftspeople in India bend and shape them into useful things.

A shoe rack

A bird cage

Recycling cans

Steel food and aluminum soda pop cans can be recycled to make new steel or aluminum.

Recycling bins

You can put both steel and aluminum cans into recycling bins. Magnets separate the steel cans at a recycling center.

Fine foil

Aluminum can be made into thin sheets of foil used for baking pans or candy wrappers. You can recycle foil, but keep it separate from cans.

YOU CAN HELP

Aluminum factories buy empty cans because they can be used again and again for making more aluminum.

Raise money for your school, a club, or a charity by collecting empty cans for recycling.

• Check that the cans are made of aluminum. They have a shiny base, whereas the base of a steel can looks dull.

• Aluminum cans are not magnetic. Test the side of a can with a magnet.

REMEMBER!

Crush cans to save space in recycling bins.

Recycling aluminum cans

1. At a recycling center, a heavy press squashes the empty pop cans together into bales.

3. The molten aluminum is poured into a **mold** and then cooled with water. The aluminum sets into a big block called an **ingot**.

4. Rollers flatten the ingot into a long sheet of very thin metal.

2. The bales go to a **foundry**, where they are shredded, cleaned, and melted in a hot furnace along with raw materials.

5. New cans are punched from the sheet. These are filled with soda pop and sent to stores.

Canny transformations

In countries where new metal is expensive, empty steel pop cans are a cheap raw material for craftworkers. They are thin and easy to cut with hand tools.

Can collection

This South African craftsman designs dozens of things from pop cans, including belts, bowls, boxes, and toys. Street children bring him more than half a million cans a year off the street. He pays for them by the bagful.

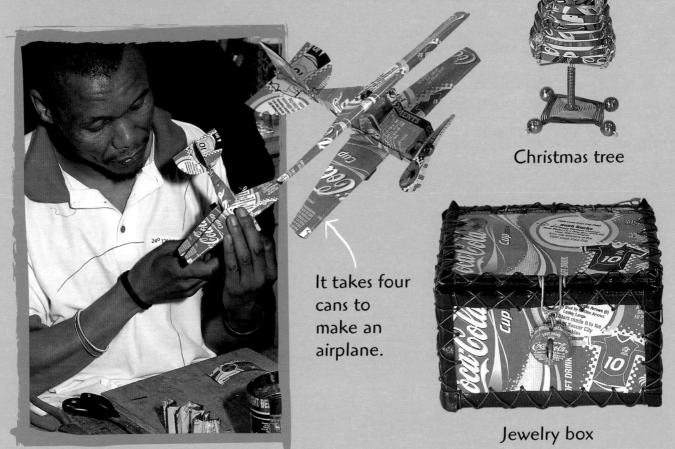

Christmas tree

It takes four cans to make an airplane.

Jewelry box

A shady visor

1. The craftsman washes the cans, cuts off the ends, and slices the cans down one side.

2. He flattens the can pieces and cuts shapes out of them using a **template**.

3. He glues on a soft fabric lining.

4. He drills holes at evenly spaced intervals along each piece of the visor.

5. He sews the pieces together with scrap telephone wire.

Steely surprises

In parts of Africa and India, people create useful objects using the strong metal from empty glue or cooking oil cans.

Money box

Festive gifts

At the festival of Id, parents give their children money. In the weeks before Id, some craftsmen in Egypt turn from making stoves and buckets to making money boxes. Parents buy them to encourage their children to save.

Parents also buy their children toys made from cut-up cans.

Rattle

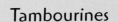

Tambourines

Kitchen equipment

Many people cannot afford new, factory-made kitchen tools. Instead, they buy cheaper ones hand-crafted from food cans.

Grater

Funnel

Kitchen tongs

Slotted spoon

Ladle

Strainer

Craftworkers also make tourist souvenirs.

Toy vehicles

Madagascans make toy vehicles from cans. Each family makes a different type, so they do not compete for sales.

Motorcycle

Car

Crafty creatures

Zimbabweans make model animals.

Airplane

19 Chameleon   Crab   Duck

Bottle tops and ring pulls

Even the metal bottle tops and ring pulls from cans are reused to make something new.

Making music

Thread the bottle tops onto a piece of metal wire. The bottle tops clink and clank when you wave this shaker back and forth.

Shaker

Curious candlesticks

A bottle top is set into each of these Indian papier mâché candleholders for a candle to stand in.

More than a dozen bottle tops make up the column of this candlestick.

A surprising suitcase

Can you figure out how many bottle tops make up this suitcase? The bottle tops are joined together with twisted wire.

One of a kind

A Brazilian bag maker threads strips of old fabric or leather through ring pulls to make bags like these. The one on the left shows the Brazilian flag.

Jangling jewelry

A Jamaican jeweler flattened bottle tops to make these colorful earrings.

Ring pulls were threaded in pairs on a strip of rubber to make this unusual bracelet.

YOUR TURN

In many parts of the world, children play checkers in the sand or on a board, using bottle tops as the game pieces.

Make your own checkers board.
- Draw a grid of 64 squares on cardboard.
- Color in alternate squares.
- Collect 24 bottle tops—it does not matter if they are not all the same.

Lay the bottle caps out to play. One player lays them top side up; the other lays them upside down.

Misprinted metal sheets

A sheet of
misprinted bottle tops

Steel cans and bottle
tops are made from large
sheets of steel. Before
a sheet is cut, the name
of a product is printed
all over it. If the name
is misprinted, the sheet
is rejected.

Metal craftsmen buy misprinted sheets very cheaply. They cut them up to make them into lamps, storage cans, and other household things.

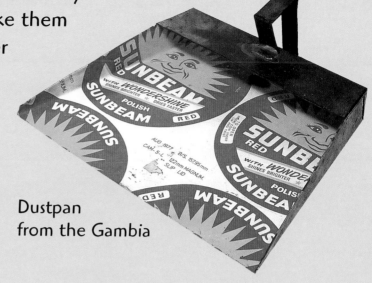

Dustpan from the Gambia

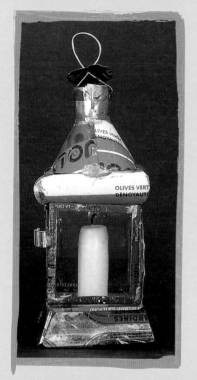

Lantern and candlestick from Morocco

Food scoop from India

Storage can from Indonesia

Watering can from Morocco

Container conversions

People send goods across the sea in shipping containers. After years of use, the huge containers are so battered by wind and waves that they are no longer usable for sea voyages. However, in South Africa, many are converted into buildings.

Changing containers

Workmen cut new windows and doors in the containers, add new flooring, and install electricity and water. Trucks transport the containers to an empty site. A crane lifts them into place.

A takeout stall

This takeout stall is a container fitted with a spit for roasting chickens, a fridge, a sink, a cupboard, and a serving window.

Township telephones

There are container phone shops on many street corners in the townships near Cape Town. Inside each one are five phone booths.

A spacious library

Three containers were joined together to make this spacious children's library.

Stacked studios

A British architect has designed apartments and studios made from containers stacked several stories high. Notice how the original doors have become the sides of the balconies.

Recycling steel

Most steel is recycled into new steel. This saves the energy used to mine and heat iron ore, and saves very useful metal as well. It also helps the **environment** because the metal is not buried at a **landfill site**.

Reduced to scrap

Millions of cars are recycled every year—much more than anything else made of metal.

Scrapyards break up the cars, stripping out any parts that can be used again.

Magnets separate the steel from other metals. The steel is then recycled.

Cars piled up in a scrapyard

Around and around

Absolutely everything made of steel contains some recycled steel. A new car may contain steel that was once part of a washing machine or a can.

When cans are recycled, the steel might be used in new cans, in a steel girder for a building, or in a refrigerator.

YOU CAN HELP

Recycle all your steel food and pet food cans and aerosols.

- *Rinse cans before recycling. Beware of any sharp edges.*

- *Put the lids inside the cans.*

- *Squash cans as flat as you can.*

REMEMBER!

- *Do NOT squash aerosols.*

- *Remove the plastic top.*

- *Put the aerosols in the recycling bins just as they are.*

aerosol

27

Glossary

aluminum a hard, light, silvery-white metal, often used to make soda pop cans and foil

bale a large bundle

blast furnace a tall tower lined with fireproof bricks where iron is melted at a very high heat

coke a fuel made by heating coal in an oven

conduct to transfer heat or electricity easily from place to place

copper a soft, brownish-red metal that does not rust

environment the world around us— the land, sea, and air

excavator a machine used for digging something out of the ground

expand to grow bigger

factory a building where things are made in large numbers using machines

foundry a building where metal is melted and made into new things

geologist someone who studies the earth's rocks, minerals, and soil

gold a pale yellow, soft, shiny metal

ingot a hard block of metal cast in a mold

iron a very common gray metal

landfill site a huge pit in the ground where crushed garbage is buried

limestone a chalky white rock

magnet an object that attracts iron or steel

melt turn from a solid to a liquid

mercury a heavy, silvery, liquid metal

mold a hollow, shaped container into which liquid metal is poured so that the metal takes on that shape when it cools and hardens

molten melted into a liquid by great heat

ore a rock that contains metals

platinum a silvery-white precious metal

scrap metal scraps of iron or other metal, only of use for remelting

silver a shiny, gray precious metal

steel a strong, durable metal made mostly from iron

template an outline shape that can be drawn around to make the same shape over and over again

thermometer an instrument for measuring how hot or cold something is

Guess what?

- Around six percent of the weight of your household garbage is metal cans.

- More than 100 billion aluminum cans are produced in the United States each year.

- Remelting aluminum uses only five percent of the energy needed to make new aluminum.

- Steel cans are often called tin cans, because they have a very thin layer of tin (another type of metal) on the inside. This prevents the cans from rusting and ruining the food inside.

Useful Web sites

http://www.aluminum.org
The official Web site of The Aluminum Association, Inc.; this site provides information about the aluminum industry and recycling

http://www.astc.org/exhibitions/rotten/rthome.htm
Learn the Rotten Truth About Garbage with interesting facts about the world's dumps and what happens to garbage

http://www.epa.gov/recyclecity/
See how Dumptown became Recycle City with fun games and interesting facts about recycling metal and other materials

http://www.olliesworld.com/planet/
A fun, interactive site that includes information and tips on recycling steel and aluminum cans

http://www.planetpals.com/earthday.html
Projects and information about Earth Day, America Recycles Day, and other events that promote recycling

http://www.recycleyourcans.org
An interactive site with games and videos, including fun facts about recycling aluminum cans and a link to local recycling centers

Index

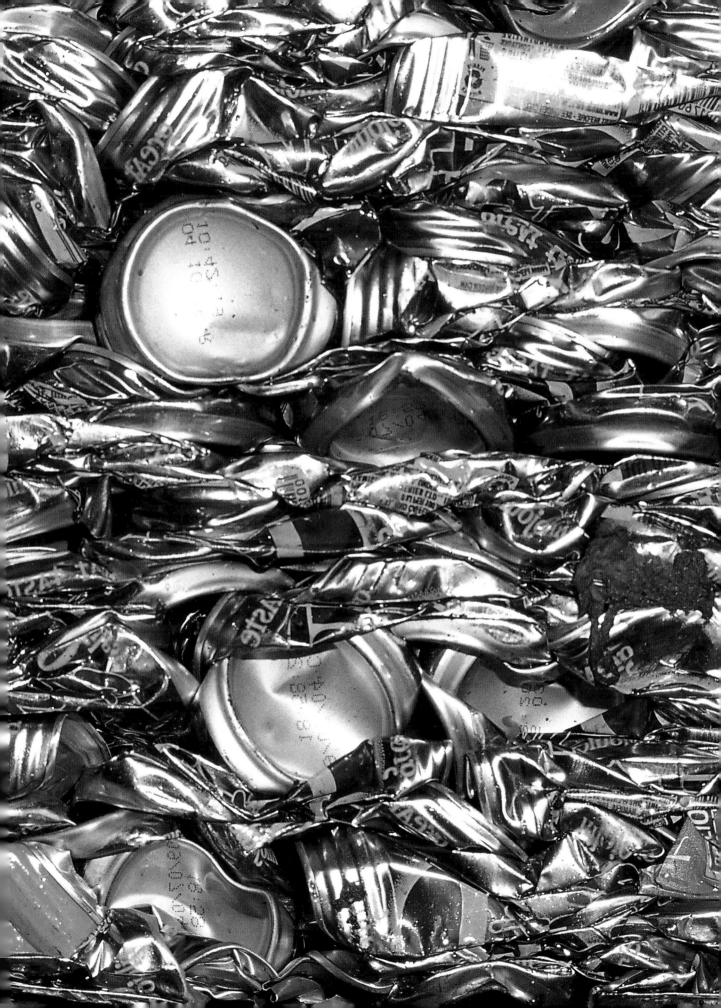